24 Hou

What Do Animals Do All Day?

by Wendy Hunt

Illustrated by Muti

WIDE EYED EDITIONS

Contents

Are you ready for an adventure?

Come with us and find out what animals do...

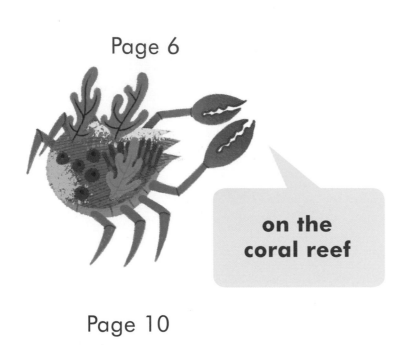

 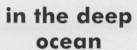

What do animals do all day?

On this trip we are going to visit 14 different habitats, and in each place we are going to talk to eight animals.

Each of the animals you meet can be seen doing their job on the page before. Can you spot them all?

Welcome to the world of animals! Our beautiful Earth has so many different places on it, each home to many kinds of creatures...

But what do they do all day?

Each animal has a special job to do that's developed to fit the place they live. In each habitat, the animals' jobs help them and their neighbours to have better lives.

Some habitats may be dry and hot, with dust that blows in your face. Other habitats may be steep and rocky, where dark evergreen trees tower. Still other habitats may lie along the beach in the ocean shallows, where salty waves splash over the animals living there.

Join us on our adventure as we visit some very different places to see what kinds of jobs animals do all day. Some of these jobs might truly surprise you!

Welcome to the coral reef

Sunshine shimmers through shallow water to touch tables and towers of coral. A rainbow of fish flutter through high arches, across underwater mountains, and into cracks in the rocks. The tropical coral reef is its own city, where every fish has a job!

I look like a kitchen SPONGE. I clean the water that flows through my body.

As a DECORATOR CRAB, I stick pieces of sponge on my shell so predators don't see me. Oooh la la!

I'm a PARROTFISH. My job is to bite off coral chunks, chew them up and poop out new sand for the reef.

I can pretend to be a lion fish, flat fish, sea snake or even a jelly fish. That's right, I'm a MIMIC OCTOPUS!

Welcome to the savannah

On the Kenyan savannah in Africa, waving grass stretches in every direction as far as you can see. Half the year is rainy, making the savannah muddy and green, and half the year is dry, with yellow grass and hot days. Animals might want to stay out of the sun then, but they've got work to do!

What do animals do on the savannah?

Like other ELEPHANTS, I change the landscape by uprooting trees and creating waterholes and wallows.

I am a WHITE RHINO. I fight other rhinos using my sharp horn. My skin is so tough it's like body armour.

I am a CHEETAH, and I can reach speeds of up to 95 kilometres per hour in 3 seconds. I'm faster than a greyhound!

I am a HIPPO. I only come out of the water at night to prune bushes, grasses or trees.

I am a SECRETARY BIRD. I hunt, stamp on and eat snakes to keep pests in check.

You better watch out for me! I'm a LION and I'm at the top of the food chain round here.

I'm always on my feet, alert to danger. GIRAFFES only sleep for 2 hours a day!

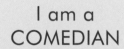

I laugh hysterically to show how important I am in the group. I am a HYENA.

Welcome to the rainforest

Tall trees, looping vines, leaves as big as your head, sheets of rain, clouds of insects – this is the tropical rainforest in Borneo. There are more kinds of plants and animals living here than anywhere else on earth. The animals who work the rainforest night shift have many different jobs.

What do animals do in the rainforest?

I am a **LONG JUMPER**

I am a **COFFEE FARMER**

Try keeping up with me as I jump from tree to tree! TARSIERS can leap 40 times their body length.

I am a CIVET. I eat berries and after they go through my digestive system, they make amazing coffee!

I am a **PALM PATROLLER**

I am a **SOUND ENGINEER**

What's that? It's a rat stealing palm nuts. I'll catch him! I'm the LEOPARD CAT palm patrol!

I'm a LARGE-EARED HORSESHOE BAT. I use sound waves and echoes to find moths in the dark.

I weave a cocoon for sleeping in. It's spiky outside, because I'm a SPIKY CATERPILLAR, but inside it's smooth.

I'm a BEARDED PIG. I run through the rainforest, watching for monkeys. They drop my favourite treat – fruit!

I like to keep an eye on everything. As a WOOD OWL, I can turn my head right round to see behind me.

I can pretend to be a leaf, but I'm actually a LONG-NOSED HORNED FROG.

Welcome to the desert

Take a breath of desert air. If the wind is blowing, fine sand might coat your tongue. If it's midday, your mouth might feel dry fast. The animals that live and work in the Sahara Desert have special ways to thrive in the heat with very little water. Let's see what some of them do for a job.

What do animals do in the desert?

I am a
TRUCKER

I'm a DROMEDARY CAMEL and I can travel for days without water. My padded feet protect me from the hot sand.

I am a
HAIRDRESSER

I'm an ANUBIS BABOON. I love doing my friends' hair, and I love it when they do mine.

I am a
TEACHER

As a GOLDEN JACKAL mum, I spend six months teaching my puppies.

I am an
EXTERMINATOR

I'm a RÜPPELL'S SAND FOX. When I eat rats and insects, I save crops and people from disease.

I have powerful legs because I'm an OSTRICH. I can even kick down a lion!

BARBARY SHEEP are very polite. We don't start to fight until our opponent is completely ready.

I'm a DEATH STALKER SCORPION. Researchers are making my venom into a cure for brain tumours.

I'm an ADDAX SCREWHORN ANTELOPE. I can detect rain from far away, and then go to find water.

Welcome to the river

One of the world's biggest rivers travels over 3,000 kilometres through the United States – the Mississippi. In some places the river is wide and lazy; in others it's narrow and speedy. All kinds of animals work on the busy Mississippi, both in the water and on its banks. But what kinds of jobs do they do?

What do animals do on the river?

I am an
ENGINEER

I am an
INNKEEPER

Welcome to my home! I'm a BALD EAGLE, and I use sticks to build the biggest single nest of any bird.

Which room would you like? I'm a MUSKRAT, and my waterfront lodge has room for other animals.

I am a
DIVER

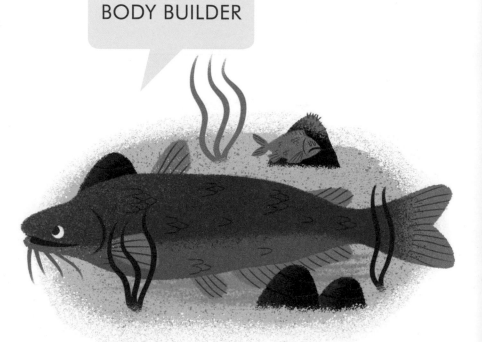

I am a
BODY BUILDER

I'm a DOUBLE-CRESTED CORMORANT. My special feathers help me dive deep to find food.

I start off little, but I'm a BLUE CATFISH, and I can grow to be heavier than 45 kilograms!

I'm a CRAYFISH. Everyone else likes to swim in the river, but I walk along the bottom instead.

I'm a SHOVELNOSE STURGEON. I use the sensitive whiskers on my nose to find food on the riverbed.

I'm a WOOD DUCK. I like to make my family's nest in trees beside the river with a waterfront view.

RIVER OTTERS have membranes over their eyes, so I can see everything under water. I don't need goggles!

Welcome to the North Pole

The name 'North Pole' might make you think of polar bears, but there are many other animals in the Arctic as well. All of these animals are used to extreme cold and lots of snow. Each of them has special tactics that let them do their jobs even when there is a blizzard.

What do animals do at the North Pole?

Like other BELUGA WHALES, I twitter and chirp to talk with my family and friends.

My POLAR BEAR cubs are the best behaved in the Arctic. They stay perfectly still while I hunt.

I love being with my friends and family. We live together in groups of ORCAS called 'pods'.

I'm a MUSK OX. The whole family takes care of our little ones. When danger threatens, we circle around them.

I am a SUNBATHER

It's so cold up here that ARCTIC WOOLLY MOTHS like me often freeze. Luckily the sun thaws me so I can fly.

I am a WINTER OLYMPIAN

I'm a SNOWSHOE HARE. I duck and dodge with my long, furry feet, moving fast if I need to!

I am a TUNNEL DIGGER

I'm an ARCTIC FOX. In a blizzard, I tunnel down into the snow to create a cosy shelter.

I am DRESSED TO IMPRESS

You won't miss me in my shiny black and white tuxedo colours. I'm a RIBBON SEAL and I look good!

29

Welcome to the mountain

In the thin air of the Swiss Alps, animals work to raise and feed their families. It's not always easy, but they move around the steep, green meadows, and leap or fly up rocky cliffs to get to where they need to be. Which animals work in this high alpine world?

What do animals do on the mountain?

I am a
STUNTMAN

I am a
COMPANION

I am a GOLDEN EAGLE. Watch me dive like a bullet to catch my prey in mid-air!

I stay with my mate all of my life in this high mountain habitat. I'm a loyal ALPINE CHOUGH.

I am a
FISHERMAN

I am a
HIGH-FLYER

I'm a BROWN BEAR and I fish many ways – reach and grab, sit and wait, underwater snorkelling and stealing!

I'm a RED APOLLO BUTTERFLY. I flutter in flowers high in the Alps, above all other butterflies.

It doesn't matter if I'm hunting, or just taking a stroll. I'm a WOLF SPIDER, and I carry my eggs along.

See my heavy, curved horns? I use them to fight other ALPINE IBEX – crash!

I'm an ALPINE MARMOT. My friends and I sit around and groom each other for hours.

Put up your paws! I dare you to punch me! I'm a BROWN HARE, and I'm a feisty boxer during the spring.

Welcome to the forest

Dark evergreens stretch their bristly arms up to the sky. They step up steep, rocky hills in Alberta, Canada. On the ground underneath the trees, and high in the branches, animals use this forest as their workplace. The taiga animals have adapted to work shifts during long, cold winters and short, warm summers.

What do animals do in the forest?

Like every BEAVER, I know exactly which trees I should cut to build my beautiful log lodge.

I'm a COUGAR. I can run fast, jump high and ambush deer when they least expect it.

I'm a FLYING SQUIRREL. My legs and arms have furry webbing between them, so I can jump from tree to tree.

I won't shoot my quills, but if you touch me, they'll come off and prick you! I'm a NORTH AMERICAN PORCUPINE.

I am a
NAVIGATOR

With my family and friends, I can find my way for over 2,000 kilometres in 24 hours. I'm a CANADA GOOSE.

I am a
CROSS-COUNTRY
SKIER

Like other CANADA LYNX, I move quickly across deep snow on my tufted, furry feet.

I am a
COMMANDO

My group of GREY WOLVES are stealthy when we hunt. We send each other noiseless signals.

I am a
PERFUMIER

I'm a STRIPED SKUNK. If I spray you with my stinky 'perfume', it will last for days!

Welcome to the plains

If you visited the Great Plains prairie, it might seem empty at first. But look a little closer, and you would see holes in the ground, mounds of dirt and insects crawling on plants. Look up, and you might see the sudden rush of wings... What kind of animals work and live on the sweeping, grassy plains?

What do animals do on the plains?

I'm a PRAIRIE DOG. I report whoever walks past our town, with special barks for people, coyotes and hawks.

My family of AMERICAN BISON have walked this land for years, followed by people who built trails, and then roads.

Yes, I'm an owl, but I'm a BURROWING OWL. I dig tunnels and live in underground hideaways.

I'm a RED JUMPING SPIDER. I knit long silk tubes to crawl inside during thunderstorms and at night.

I'm a PRONGHORN. I run and run... and run! I can keep on running at 40 kilometres per hour for ages.

My PRAIRIE CHICKEN courting dance is a grand show – fancy footwork, snapping tail and booming song.

I collect extra snacks in my cheek pockets while I dig tunnels with my big teeth. I'm a POCKET GOPHER.

I live on the plains in winter, but fly up to the Arctic each summer. That's why I'm called a SNOW GOOSE.

Welcome to a tropical island

The Hawaiian Islands sit alone in the middle of the Pacific Ocean. Some animals here have always been here. Others are from somewhere else – brought here by people years ago. They've settled down to raise families and do their jobs. The original 'Hawaiians' and the newcomers work side by side.

43

What do animals do on a tropical island?

I am a NANNY

I'm a HAWAIIAN MONK SEAL. I don't only raise my own pups, I care for other seal pups too.

I am a HIGH JUMPER

Like other MANTA RAYS, I leap three metres out of the water and flap my wings before splashing down.

I am a GARDENER

Sea grass grows much thicker after GREEN SEA TURTLES like me nibble the tip of each grass blade.

I am a BURGLAR

I'm an AFRICAN WILD ASS, and I get thirsty in this heat! I'll just sneak into this garden and have some pool water...

Mmmm. I do love eggs! I'll need to be quiet as I reach into this nest . . . luckily I'm a super sneaky INDIAN MONGOOSE.

I'm a HAWAIIAN HOARY BAT. I chase mosquitoes, gnats and any other insects that might bother you.

My great-grandparents were brought to the zoo, but they escaped! Now I roam free with other ROCK WALLABIES.

I'm an ALBATROSS. I spread my wings wide, catch the wind and glide for hours without flapping once.

Welcome to the wetlands

These watery reed beds are found in Somerset. The sky above is work and home to many birds, like thousands of starlings, who fly together in perfect unity. In the water nearby more animals are doing their jobs in this wet habitat.

What do animals do in the wetlands?

I am a
SLEIGH-RIDER

I'm a playful OTTER! I like to slide down slippery muddy banks, using my body as a sleigh.

I am an
AEROBATIC
FLYER

I swoop, climb, dive and soar exactly together with thousands of my fellow STARLINGS.

I am a
CAMPER

I'm a caterpillar. In winter, I roll in a leaf to hibernate before becoming a WHITE ADMIRAL BUTTERFLY.

I am a
TRAPEZE
ARTIST

I can hang upside down with ease all day long, because I'm a LESSER HORSESHOE BAT.

I am a SUN SEEKER

Brrrr! I'm a MARSH BANDIT and I hate the cold, so I always fly to Africa for winter.

I am a SUBMARINER

What? I can't hear you. I'm a WATER VOLE and I have built-in earplugs that keep out water when I go deep.

I am an OPERA SINGER

I might look small and brown, but I'm a CETTI'S WARBLER, and my beautiful song may stop you in your tracks.

I am a SYNCHRONISED SWIMMER

I'm a GREAT CRESTED GREBE. I perform a fancy swimming dance to win the heart of my lady love.

Welcome to the mangroves

Mangrove forests in Indonesia aren't like anywhere else – an in-between place where ocean and land mix. Mangrove trees drink salt water through their roots, while their branches reach high in the humid air. As they filter the water, mangroves provide a work place to many animals, large and small.

What do animals do in the mangroves?

I'm a MUDSKIPPER. Most fish think dry land is a different planet, but I can go there, using my water-filled sacs to breathe.

I'm a FIDDLER CRAB. I gobble up sand, sift out the food to eat, and sculpt sand balls out of the leftovers.

I'm a PROBOSCIS MONKEY. I love climbing high in the mangrove trees and diving into the water.

As a male SNOWY EGRET, I do a fancy dance to get the ladies to look at me.

I'm called TOKAY GECKO because at night I yell, "Tokay! Tokay!", and everyone knows everything is normal.

I crawl down branches when the tide is down, and slide back up before it rises. I am a MANGROVE SNAIL.

I'm a MANGROVE BAT, and I chew mangrove leaves to make them tip together into the perfect tent.

Silent and deadly, I drop down on my prey out of the trees. I'm a MANGROVE CAT SNAKE.

Welcome to the deep ocean

Humans can't survive here, except in special vehicles. It's dark, cold, and lifeless... Wait! There – in the shadows – a pinpoint of green light. And another line of lights in the dark! There is life down here. In the deepest ocean, animals go about their jobs in the cold darkness.

What do animals do in the deep ocean?

I am an IMPRESSIONIST

I am a FISHING TRAWLER

You may have to look twice – I'm really a FRILLED SHARK even though I move like a snake.

I'm a GULPER EEL. My huge mouth scoops in small fish for me to eat.

I am a DEEP-SEA DIVER

I am a COUCH POTATO

No fish in the ocean swims deeper than me! I'm a FANGTOOTH FISH.

It's easy to see why I'm a BLOBFISH. I have no muscles, I have no bones and I hardly ever move!

When I pull my arms up, the webbing between them drapes in a dark cloak. That's why I'm called a VAMPIRE SQUID.

I'm a PACIFIC VIPERFISH. I have a fishing light in front of my mouth to lure prey.

I'm an ELECTRIC STARGAZER. I lie just beneath the sand with my wide mouth open, ready to trap prey.

I dance through the deeps by gently flapping my 'ears'. That's why I'm called a DUMBO OCTOPUS.

Welcome to the garden

When you open your back door and go outside, you are entering an animal habitat. Look around. What animals and insects would you see if you lived in Washington state? What are they doing? Just like people working at different jobs, the animals in your garden are working to feed their families and make their lives better.

What do animals do in the garden?

I am a HANDYMAN

I am a FARMHAND

I'm a RACCOON. I study new things by touching them and turning them around in my hands.

Farmers love me since I target pests in the fields. I'm a LADYBIRD.

I am an ACTOR

I am a FAST FOOD FANATIC

I half close my eyes, froth at the mouth, and lie very still. You may think I'm dead, but I'm just a play-acting POSSUM.

Hurry! Eat that quick, before a cougar comes! We're DEER, so our other stomachs can digest it later.

I am a CORRESPONDENT

After I forage, I pass on news to other HONEY BEES of where to find pollen and nectar by dancing.

I am a GYMNAST

I'm a SLUG. I can stretch and bend 20 times my length to get wherever I need to go.

I am a HOARDER

Like other CHIPMUNKS, I collect so much food all summer, I can doze and snack all winter.

I am a PILOT

I hover, I turn, I dive, I dip – I'm a HUMMINGBIRD, and I can handle any flying challenge.

Index of animals

Brimming with creative inspiration, how-to projects, and useful information to enrich your everyday life, Quarto Knows is a favourite destination for those pursuing their interests and passions. Visit our site and dig deeper with our books into your area of interest: Quarto Creates, Quarto Cooks, Quarto Homes, Quarto Lives, Quarto Drives, Quarto Explores, Quarto Gifts, or Quarto Kids.

First published in 2018 by Wide Eyed Editions, an imprint of The Quarto Group. The Old Brewery, 6 Blundell Street, London N7 9BH, United Kingdom. T (0)20 7700 6700 F (0)20 7700 8066 www.QuartoKnows.com

ISBN 978-1-84780-971-1

The illustrations were created digitally
Set in Futura

Published by Jenny Broom and Rachel Williams
Designed by Karissa Santos
Edited by Jenny Broom and Katie Cotton
Production by Jenny Cundill

Manufactured in Dongguan, China TL 102017

9 8 7 6 5 4 3 2 1